To Do Lists That Wo

You've been making lists your whole life.

Planning a birthday party? Make a list of people to invite, food to make, and games to play.

Going shopping? Make a list of everything you need to buy.

Going on holidays? Make a list of things to pack, and another list of activities to do while you're away.

That same advice extends to to do lists. It's considered good practice to make and maintain a list of all the tasks you need to do. You may even have a separate list for things to do at work and things to do at home. Of course, as you get busier and take on more responsibilities, your to do lists continue to grow.

Before long, your to do lists have spiralled out of control, and the list is no longer serving its purpose. No longer is your to do list a useful tool to help keep you organised and reduce your mental clutter. Now your lists represent a mountain of tasks that no one could hope to complete in a lifetime.

As to do lists become more complicated, new problems emerge. How do you prioritise the various items on your list? Is it better to start with the easiest tasks every day? You'll get the short-term satisfaction of striking out four or five items from your list. But when will you start the harder, longer, or more complicated tasks? If you devote your energy to a longer or harder task, when will you tackle the smaller, admin-style tasks?

It's impossible to write a to do list without considering broader time management issues. The way you write your to do lists and the level of priority you give each item determines how you manage your time. Prioritising simpler tasks comes at the cost of larger, difficult, or ongoing tasks.

What if everything you've learned about time management and to do lists is wrong? What if there's a better way of managing your time, keeping track of your tasks, and prioritising your workload? What if you never needed to write a to do list again?

There is such a way, and it involves using an item that almost everyone uses anyway. In fact, you've probably used this item at least once already today, whether in paper or digital format. Almost every family has one hanging on their wall or on the fridge.

What is it?

A calendar.

Here's what you can expect from this book:

Learn how successful people manage their time and keep track of their tasks.

- Find out why the world's most successful people don't keep to do lists.
- See first-hand how successful people track their time using an everyday calendar.
- Discover step-by-step methods to use your calendar to schedule everything.
- Learn how to prioritise every single task on your list.
- Find diagrams, illustrations, worked examples, and calendar templates.
- Make the transition from unmanageable to do lists to a perfectly organised calendar.

None of the ideas in this book are new. There is no app to buy, and no equipment you'll need other than whatever calendar or planner you already use. There is also no follow-up course, seminar, or training program. This book includes everything you need to transition from a to do list to a calendar system. There is no sales pitch, no email list to sign up for, and nothing else you'll need to do. This book contains worked examples, step-by-step instructions, and all the templates you need.

Are you ready to follow the example of the world's most successful and productive people? Then let's get started, moving away from to do lists and towards a simpler calendar system.

Essential Ideas to Understand

We're almost ready to find out how to get rid of your to do list forever and move to a calendar system. But first, there are some essential ideas you need to understand. Let's get the foundation out of the way and move on to the substantive part of this book.

What Are You Trying To Achieve?

There's something you need to do before you can design your ideal calendar workflow. First, you need to work out what it is that you're trying to achieve.

Taking the time to answer this question will serve two important purposes:

1) Your answers will help you delegate or delete tasks that don't help you achieve your goals.
2) You'll find enhanced motivation to tackle the tasks that are in line with your goals.

Why is this question so important? Because there are so many different tasks and distractions competing for your attention. It's easy to get so caught up with emails, meetings, appointments, and admin tasks that you lose the big picture.

There is a world of information about goal setting, and we won't reinvent the wheel here. The important point is to work out your "big picture", keep it in mind, and test each task against it. Before committing to any task, you have to know why you want to complete the task. Which of your goals does the task align with?

A good way to start is to consider what your ideal work week would look like.

- Are you a freelancer? Most of your ideal workday might be set aside for completing and delivering work. You also need time for communicating with clients and invoicing. Don't forget growing your client base by quoting on new work and self-promoting.
- Are you an employee? The bulk of your week is likely made up with assigned work. You'll also need time for meetings, new lead acquisitions, and administrative tasks.
- Do you split your time between employment and raising children or running a house? Your work week will be a delicate mix of family time, your children's commitments, and your work tasks.

Everyone's lives and jobs are different. Your ideal work week will never look the same as someone else's. But I'll bet nobody's list includes hours sifting through old emails or browsing social media.

Let's take an example. You're a freelance writer with the following ideal work week breakdown:

- 60% client work
- 20% new client acquisition
- 10% communicating with existing clients
- 10% administrative and financial tasks.

You're running late on a project and have spent the whole day on client work. You have one hour of working time left in the day and two items on your to do list vying for your attention. What do you do?

1) Complete a long and involved application for an exciting new project, or
2) Update social media with your latest completed projects and comment on related posts.

The social media task is the easiest and most enjoyable of the two. But what are you trying to achieve? Before choosing the social media admin tasks to round out your day, go back to your ideal work week. Ask yourself: why you would want to complete either of the tasks? Because it's the easier choice, or because it better aligns with your goals?

Your choice becomes clear. Although the project application is a more difficult task, it's also more rewarding. The project application fits into the 20% time allocated to new client acquisition. Social media updates form part of the 10% allowed for admin and financial tasks. Your career depends on you bringing in new clients and new projects. The project application becomes the best choice.

Prioritising your time and creating your calendar relies on these kinds of decisions. Your ability to make these decisions will increase once you:

- Have set your goals
- Know what you're trying to achieve
- Understand what your ideal work week looks like.

Your To Do List Will Never Be Complete

Keep in mind that your to do list will never be complete. There will always be new tasks added to your list. Oftentimes the number of new tasks added is greater than the number of tasks completed each day. The aim should never be to check off every item on your to do list. It isn't possible.

This is what sets to do lists apart from other kinds of lists.

If you're planning an event, you may make a list of all the tasks you need to complete to make the event a success. You'll aim to complete all these tasks before the event occurs. The same is true for a shopping list or a vacation packing list.

Your to do list represents something different. It describes how you spend your days, and how you prioritise your time. It is your job description, your set of responsibilities.

Would you even want to check off every item on your to do list? What happens then?

We're taught to feel dissatisfied when our list still exists after crossing off items all day. We groan as we add new items to the list.

It's so important to understand that your to do list will always keep growing and will never be "finished".

Now you can:

- Do away with the false assumption that the list will soon disappear
- Stop treating each item as equal
- Focus on prioritising and spending your time in the best way.

Productivity, or the Feeling of Productivity?

It's an easy trap to fall into. How often do you spend time on tasks that make you feel productive but which don't take you any closer to your goals? This idea circles back to the previous idea of goal-setting and knowing what you want to achieve.

Let's go back to the example of the freelance writer with one hour to spare. You could apply for a new project that, if successful, would create six months work. But, you argue, doing this:

- Will take the full hour
- Requires you to provide detailed answers about your qualifications and experience
- May not earn you any new work, or even prompt an acknowledgement of your application.

From that point of view, there is every reason to not start the application at all.

But you allocated 20% of your ideal work week to new client acquisition. You did that for a reason. Let's go over those arguments again:

- "The application will take the full hour." - You'd be spending that time at work anyway. You may as well put it to good use rather than wasting it. Your success as a freelancer hinges on bringing new clients and new projects on board.
- "The application requires you to provide detailed answers about your qualifications and experience." - While you may not get this project, the application you create will help you apply for future projects.
- "You may not get any new work, or even an acknowledgement of your application." - There's always the risk of a wasted application, but you won't get any new work if you don't apply.

Creating the application may not be an exciting task to work on in the short term, but you recognise that applying for new projects is a vital part of your success as a freelancer.

Or you could spend that same hour sorting through your inbox. You've been busy with client projects and have 200+ emails demanding your attention. In that hour you could reduce the overload by deleting spam, ads, and newsletters. You could note upcoming appointments and reply to simple emails. One hour later you'd have less than 20 crucial emails that you'll later create detailed replies to.

In the short term, how would it feel to reduce your inbox from 200 down to 20?

- You'd get an enormous sense of short-term satisfaction.
- You would have the all-important feeling of busyness and of being productive.
- You'd have a valid answer should anyone ask you how you spent the last hour of the work day.

These feelings can be enticing. That's why it's so important to understand this crucial truth.

Tasks that give us a short-term feeling of productivity are often not ones that take us closer to our goals.

The same is true for meetings. Many of the world's most successful and powerful people say, "No" to all but the most crucial meetings. On the rare occasion they agree to a meeting, they set a clear and strict time limit. They'll also only attend once the organiser has reduced the agenda and aim to writing.

Successful people know that meetings are an excellent way to feel busy and important. But meeting are usually far from productive.

Develop an awareness of the difference between:

- A short-term feeling of productivity, and
- The discomfort that often accompanies tasks that take us towards our desired goals.

Rather than focusing on how you feel during the task, look ahead a few hours to when you're evaluating your day.

Imagine this scenario. You're the freelance writer again. It's the end of the day, and you're lying in bed thinking about your day.

- If you had chosen to to sort through your emails for the last hour of the day, how would you feel? The feelings of busyness that you experienced at the time would be long gone. That project application still looms large on your to do list. You'd feel regret for not having completed it.
- If you had chosen to spend that hour applying for the new project, how would you feel? The short-term discomfort and hard work would be long forgotten. You'd feel like you made the most of your limited working time and ended your day on a high.

Why To Do Lists Fail, According to Science

A to do list is nothing more than a tool to help you keep track of all the tasks currently on your plate. Like any tool, its success depends on how you set it up and how you use it. No to do list is ever going to complete the tasks for you. And a to do list that isn't used - no matter how well you've put it together - is worth less than the paper it's written on.

But even the best to do list can make it difficult to complete your tasks and be productive. We won't go into the psychology and science behind these reasons. Instead, let's summarise the reasons why a to do list could make it difficult to be productive.

- A sense of overwhelm from seeing the growing list of tasks on your to do list.
- The feeling of disappointment that no matter how hard you work each day, most of the items will remain. This feeling stems from the erroneous belief that we should aim to complete every item on our to do list.
- A lack of prioritising, causing you to view basic admin tasks with the same importance as a major project. You then spend a disproportionate amount of time working on basic tasks to see them crossed off the list. Meanwhile, you're neglecting tasks of critical importance.
- A sense of confusion from having tasks from different areas of your life mixed together. When you're at work, seeing home chores on your to do list can cause confusion and overwhelm.
- Disappointment and overwhelm as you add new items faster than you check off completed items.

To do lists fail because they appear to represent the tasks that you must complete at a given moment. As you will soon discover, using a calendar solves this problem. A calendar represents the passage of time as a fluid concept. It makes sense to add new items to a calendar as you experience each day in a continuous pattern. A calendar has no beginning and no end. This captures the concept that time never stands still. Lists can be better used to represent a subset of tasks that will come to an end. Perfect examples include a shopping list or list of tasks to plan an event. Each of these lists has a defined end. It makes sense to aim to complete these lists.

We will explore the benefits of using a calendar instead of a to do list in greater detail later in the book.

Urgent Versus Important

For people still using a to do list, making the distinction between urgent and important is a crucial one. Ask yourself: are you willing to let other people's priorities dominate your to do list?

Suppose you receive an email from a colleague. They've dropped the ball on a project and need some data from you to finish their report on time. Meanwhile, you're working on your own project that isn't due for several weeks. You've been working on it every day so that you can produce your best work.

It can be easy to be reactive and jump into action when the task seems urgent. The email from your colleague is an urgent one, since their request from you is time sensitive. At this point you need to make the distinction between urgent and important. Your own project, while not currently urgent, is still of great importance.

What would happen if you drop your own work and help your colleague meet their deadline? You'll feel very busy and important at the time. But you'd have regrets later in the day when you realise you didn't make any progress on your own important task. Instead, you spent the day dealing with someone else's urgent priority. Your colleague made it seem like their work was important, when it was only urgent. It didn't help you reach your goals.

Most emails you receive relate to other people's urgent tasks. People try their best to present their tasks as important to you. Yet very few of them will be important from your point of view. It's tempting to spend your time reacting to tasks that seem time sensitive and urgent. Doing so makes you forever delay items which are important to you.

This is the primary reason why people fail to achieve personal goals. A goal like writing a book or learning an instrument is important. But it can't compete with the barrage of urgent tasks that demand attention.

Not distinguishing between urgent and important causes to do lists to fail. It is this distinction that makes relying on a calendar a far more productive option. A calendar system allows you to allocate non-negotiable time to important tasks. No longer will you spend your day putting out other people's fires.

The Importance of Saying "No"

When you study the habits of successful people, you'll find several recurring themes. One is that they have learned to say, "No" to almost everything. This ties back to the difference between urgent and important. Important tasks are usually tasks for yourself, like long-term goals or projects. Urgent tasks usually benefit someone else.

Think back to the colleague requesting data from you to finalise their own project. The project was important to your colleague, but not to you. Your colleague then attempted to pass on some of the work by presenting it as urgent.

You've come to this book because you're struggling with your current to do list. You're looking for a better way to manage the increasing list of tasks before you. We've talked about prioritising so easier tasks don't take precedence over harder projects. We've talked about not letting other people's priorities come before your important tasks.

The higher-level concept is to recognise the importance of saying, "No". Of course, if you're an employee, you won't have the luxury of saying "No" when your employer assigns you a task. This is true even if the task fit the definition of "urgent" at the expense of your more important tasks. As an employee, your hands are somewhat tied. But remember that part of your role as an employee is to complete tasks as assigned. If you don't, you risk losing your job. Doesn't this now give the tasks a new level of importance?

As a freelancer or consultant, you may have more freedom to say "No" to projects that don't meet your goals. But there comes a time when a decent income and the ability to pay your bills trumps your desire to say, "No" .

The more successful and powerful a person is, the more freedom they have to be picky about what to agree to. But everyone still has some freedom to say, "No". This applies to entry-level employees, students, and a freelancer starting out.

Earlier in this book we talked about:

- Understanding what you're trying to achieve
- Picturing what your ideal work week looks like
- Assigning a percentage to each of the elements of your work week.

When any new opportunity or request arises that you do have the power to say, "No" to, ask yourself this question. "How does this fit within the model I created of my ideal work week?"

Granted, you may not have much freedom to say, "No" to a new work project. But you could say, "No" to a request for after-work drinks with a former colleague, for example. That time might be better spent with your close friends or family, or exercising, or on a long-term project.

These types of choices can come up in minuscule ways, like when checking your emails. You're always making choices, even if it seems like you're running on autopilot:

- Reading a newsletter or catalogue
- Answering a survey
- Clicking an ad from a retailer you once purchased from
- Watching a YouTube video or reading an article sent by a friend.

You always have the power to say, "No" in these situations, delete the email, and move on to the next. Better yet, click "Unsubscribe" so you're not forced to make the same decision again in the future.

As you become more successful, more people will vie for your time and attention. People will want you to mentor them, collaborate with you, or interview you. You have limited time every day, and limited days in your lifetime. Be wary of so readily giving away your time. Work towards the day when you can save your "Yes" for people and opportunities that excite you.

Successful People Rely on Their Calendars

Before I wrote a word of this book, I spent months on an in-depth (some might say excessive) study. I looked into the ways different people from different walks of life all over the world kept their to do lists. I knew that most people struggled to create a focused and helpful to do list. I knew people were feeling frustrated and overwhelmed by their to do list systems. I knew that there had to be "to do lists that worked" - hence the name of this book - used by the world's most successful people.

I didn't want to reinvent the wheel and devise yet another to do list method or app to add to the confusion. Instead, I intended to find the pattern of success.

My believed that the world's most successful and productive people use a variation of the same to do list system. I intended to find that system and simplify it for everyone to use.

What I found was completely unexpected and caused me to wonder if I should choose a new title for this book. I was correct that the world's most successful people use a similar method. The method kept them organised and on top of their tasks for each day, week, month, and in the long-term. But what blew my mind was that they weren't using a to do list at all.

Successful people do not write to do lists. Successful people work from their calendars. But it's not only work - successful people live and work from their calendars.

Why did I stick with the working title for this book, "To Do Lists That Work"? Because I know that people around the world are struggling.

- Bouncing from one to do list method to the next
- Watching their frustration levels soar as their to do lists keep growing
- Never feeling like they're on top of their workload
- Tired of wrestling their cluttered and confusing to do list into something manageable.

People are looking for the to do list system that works.

Here it is. But as it turns out, it's not a to do list at all.

Successful people do not work from a list of everything they need to do. Successful people use a calendar to break their days into 15-minute intervals.

The world's most successful and productive people schedule everything. They live by the same mantra, whether they realise it or not.

"If it's not in the calendar, it won't get done."

With the foundation ideas out of the way, here's what you can expect from the rest of this book.

- How to turn your to do list into the calendar system used by the world's most successful people.
- Maintaining your new calendar system in a way that best benefits you.
- Case studies showing how different people have transitioned to the calendar system.

The Step-By-Step Method To Creating To Do Lists That Work

One-Time Steps

There's one thing you need to do before you can reap the benefits of a calendar system. First, you need to transition from your current to do list to the calendar system.

Here's the good news:

- All you have to do is follow the steps listed here.

- You only have to complete these steps once.

Let's get started!

Write Your Goal/Mission Statement

Let's start with the big picture. Before you can start blocking time into your calendar, you need a goal or mission statement. This will be the yardstick against which you measure every task.

Your time is a limited resource. Nothing makes it onto your calendar without first passing the test. You will learn to ask:

- Why is the task important?
- What am I doing it for?
- Why does it deserve a spot in my calendar?
- Why should I give up a chunk of my valuable time for it?

Your goal or mission statement will help you answer these questions in a split second.

Do you already have a goal or mission statement? Write it out again, review it, and make sure it still applies to your current circumstances.

If you don't already have a goal or mission statement, now is the time to create one.

This is not a book about goal setting. I don't want to attempt to summarise other people's much more extensive work on the topic. Reading books on goal setting will help you create your own mission statement. Stephen R Covey is an expert on the topic and has published several books.

A quicker method is to use a free online tool that guides you into creating a mission statement. I recommend Stephen Covey's free tool https://msb.franklincovey.com/. A quick online search will help you find other similar tools.

A mission statement or goal need not be complicated or all-encompassing. Try not to get too caught up in this step. If you don't have a mission statement, stop now and write something down.

In its simplest form, your mission statement or goal is your "why". It is the standard against which you measure your tasks to see if they are worth your time.

Creating a goal or mission statement at this stage is essential, but it doesn't need to be complicated.

Let's stop here and introduce out first case study. Charlie agreed to work through the steps in this book and write down their progress along the way. Watching Charlie transition from to do list to a calendar will help you see these steps in action.

Charlie, 31, parent/freelancer

In My Own Words

"I'm a single parent with two school-age kids. I work as a freelance graphic designer. I have full custody of my children so I can only work during school hours. Sometimes I can squeeze in a couple of hours on weekends depending on what we're doing. Freelancing suits my lifestyle, allowing me to work on my own terms and in my own time. My family comes first and I'm always there for them, even if it means having fewer hours to work each week."

Current To Do List System

"It's a mess more than anything else! I keep all the kids appointments and classes in my calendar, but I tend to keep most of my client work in my head. I've tried writing down due dates and other work deadlines, but the list never seems complete so I don't rely on it.

I have a mental picture of where all my projects are at and when they're due. Sometimes this means waking up in a panic since I've forgotten something due that day. I know I need to be more organised and have a better system for tracking everything.

Sometimes I get so overwhelmed with my limited working time that I end up sabotaging myself. I'll spend an hour scrolling through social media or doing housework and ruin my day."

Write Your Goal/Mission Statement

"To be the best parent I can be, and to always be there for my kids when they need me. To work as hard and smart as I can during my working hours, but not let my work spill over into time with my kids. They'll be grown up before I know it and I want to make the most of this time while they're young.

At work, I'd love to grow the logo design side of my business as much as possible. General graphic design tasks are fine, but my goal is to establish myself as an expert logo designer. I'd like to reduce the amount of time I spend on other projects. Soon I won't take on any other projects and will be 100% logo design. I'll be a a one-stop shop for companies of any size who need the perfect logo."

Work Out Your Not-Negotiables

The calendars of highly successful people all reflect a set of not-negotiables. Rather than working all hours, most successful people keep strict working hours. Except if they're travelling, successful people put strict limits on their time. It's not unusual for a CEO to always be home in time for dinner, or to never miss their child's weekend sports events. Successful people also prioritise sleep. They know how many hours they need to perform at their peak.

Now it's time for you to work out your non-negotiables. You won't be marking anything in your calendar yet - for now you're writing a list.

Consider these examples to work out which apply to you, and add others as needed.

Sleep

How many hours of sleep do you need to function?

If you've been going to bed too late and getting up too early you may not remember how it feels to wake up refreshed.

If you're unsure, start with seven or eight hours and experiment over a few weeks. Soon you'll find an amount of sleep that lets you wake up without that horrible dazed feeling.

To further complicate things, the time that you go to sleep and the time you wake up are important. In fact, your sleep health depends on both the number of hours you sleep and the actual hours you keep. Sleeping for eight hours from 3:00 a.m. to 11:00 a.m. is not the same as eight hours from 10:00 p.m. to 6:00 a.m.

If you don't know the right sleep pattern for you, make a good guess and experiment over the next few weeks.

Working Hours   9- 6. -

Work, sleep, repeat. Does it sometimes seem that you spend all your time in this pattern? Now that you've scheduled your sleep times, it's time to be very clear on your working hours.

As mentioned, successful people keep strict working hours. They know they have to fit all their work commitments into those hours.

Have you heard of Parkinson's Law, penned by C. Northcote Parkinson?

"Work expands to fill the time available for its completion."

In other words, if you have an hour to complete a task, you'll most likely get it done within the hour. If the same task had a three-week deadline, you would probably take almost the full three weeks to complete it.

It sounds counter intuitive, but having set work times helps you be more productive. Knowing you're finishing at a set time will motivate you to complete your work within this time.

There will always be more work to do. Choosing a finishing time and sticking to it helps you to set realistic goals for what you can achieve in a day.

Exercise

Exercise is one of the first things pushed aside when schedules get busy. If exercise is important to you, it needs to go on your non-negotiable list.

 Write down when you want to exercise, how often, and for how long. Whether it's a regular yoga or spin class, a certain number of days per week at the gym, or a run every morning, write it down.

Partner

If you're in a relationship, you know how important it is to schedule time for your partner. That weekly date night sounds great in theory, but it will never happen if you both don't make it a priority.

Children

If you're a parent, you'll know all too well how fleeting the years are. Before long, your children will stop begging to spend time with you and you'll be the one chasing them.

Think about the relationship you want to build with your children. What does this look like on a daily basis?

- Do you want to be there to pick them up from school each day?
- Are evening meals together a not-negotiable?
- Will you commit to helping with homework and attending sporting classes?

Decide now on the commitments you want to make to your children. Then convert this into actual times and days and write it all down.

Family and Friends

Too many people complain of losing once-valued friendships. Usually this happens because one or both of you didn't make the effort to keep in touch. You may have relatives you wish you made more of an effort with.

If you're feeling a twinge of guilt, recognise that it is quick tasks that are easiest to push from one day to the next.

- A weekly phone call home to your parents
- A monthly visit to your aunt and uncle
- Writing a note and printing some photos for your grandparents
- Replying to a letter or email filled with news from home

These are all tasks that won't happen unless you prioritise them.

Meals

Have you ever:

- Had coffee for breakfast because you overslept after staying up late?
- Skipped lunch because you were racing to finish a project on time?
- Made do with a muesli bar or couple of biscuits for lunch because you had back-to-back meetings?

When you don't nourish your body, your brain function, energy levels, and mood all suffer. Consider the meal schedule that works best for you and write down the times and duration of each.

Self-Care

What relaxes you? What makes you feel rejuvenated? What do you look forward to?

- A relaxing bubble bath with no interruptions
- Time to read the newspaper during breakfast
- A weekly massage
- Golf on Sundays

- A monthly hair appointment
- Thirty minutes to read in peace before bed.

Whatever self-care looks like for you, write it down.

Work-Specific
Depending on your work situation, you may have work-specific not-negotiables in your list.

- If you manage a team or have mentees, do you value a daily or weekly meeting or phone call?
- Does reading the latest journal articles help you perform at work?

Remember, at this stage we're talking about tasks that align with your values and goals. We're not talking about mandatory work tasks. We'll get to those later.

Long-Term Goals
Your long-term goals may be work-related or personal.

- Have you promised yourself you'll learn to play the guitar, but never seem to find the time to practice?
- Do you berate yourself every week that you didn't spend any time working on your novel or memoir?
- Are your crafting supplies gathering dust despite promising yourself you'd find time?

If there's a long-term goal you're passionate about, write it down.

- How often will you commit to working on it? Once a week? Every day?
- How long should each session last, and what time of day is best? First thing in the morning when you've got the house to yourself? Sunday evenings when everyone else is relaxing in front of the TV?

Charlie, 31, parent/freelancer

Work Out Your Not-Negotiables

Sleep

"7 hours from 10:00 p.m. to 5:00 a.m. This gives me a couple of hours to myself after the kids go to bed. I'll also get about an hour to get ready in peace in the morning before I start helping the kids get ready for school."

Working Hours

"9:00 a.m. to 2:45 p.m. each school day."

Exercise

"Spin class from 6:00 p.m. to 7:00 p.m. on Tuesdays and Thursdays. The kids can go to the creche at the gym."

Children

"My number one priority. Before school, after school, weekends - they're my focus."

Family and Friends

"I'm going to make more of an effort to catch up with friends from high school and the other parents from baby group. I'll go down to the coffee shop near the beach every Sunday morning for a few hours. The kids and I can have breakfast and they can play on the playground. I'll let everyone know that's where I'll be every week, and people will join me if they wish - with or without kids. This could be a great way for the kids to have play dates with other kids from school as well."

Meals

"Breakfast and dinner are already part of our routine. I often skip lunch because I'm racing around trying to get everything done during school hours. I'll commit to cooking an extra serving of dinner so I can have a ready-prepared meal for lunch the next day."

Self-Care

"I read every night in bed, and I'll make sure that continues. I'll put it down for 30 minutes even though I'm usually asleep 10 or 15 minutes after I start!"

Create The Basic Outline Of Your Calendar

With the information you've already written down, it's time to start with your new calendar. Below is a calendar template to guide you. Either digital or paper planners will work. Make sure you choose one that divides the day into 15-minute intervals.

If you already use a paper planner or digital calendar, feel free to keep using it. You're more likely to stick to your new system if it comes in a form you're familiar with. Otherwise, use this template to create your calendar in a document or spreadsheet.

Once you've created the outline, start blocking in the non-negotiables you identified above.

Time	Mon	Tue	Wed	Thurs	Fri	Sat	Sun
12:00 am							
12:15							
12:30							
12:45							
1:00 am							
1:15							
1:30							
1:45							
2:00 am							
2:15							
2:30							
2:45							
3:00 am							
3:15							
3:30							
3:45							
4:00 am							
4:15							
4:30							
4:45							
5:00 am							
5:15							
5:30							
5:45							
6:00 am							
6:15							
6:30							
6:45							
7:00 am							
7:15							
7:30							
7:45							

Time	Mon	Tue	Wed	Thurs	Fri	Sat	Sun
8:00 am							
8:15							
8:30							
8:45							
9:00 am							
9:15							
9:30							
9:45							
10:00 am							
10:15							
10:30							
10:45							
11:00 am							
11:15							
11:30							
11:45							
12:00 pm							
12:15							
12:30							
12:45							
1:00 pm							
1:15							
1:30							
1:45							
2:00 pm							
2:15							
2:30							
2:45							
3:00 pm							
3:15							
3:30							
3:45							

Time	Mon	Tue	Wed	Thurs	Fri	Sat	Sun
4:00 pm							
4:15							
4:30							
4:45							
5:00 pm							
5:15							
5:30							
5:45							
6:00 pm							
6:15							
6:30							
6:45							
7:00 pm							
7:15							
7:30							
7:45							
8:00 pm							
8:15							
8:30							
8:45							
9:00 pm							
9:15							
9:30							
9:45							
10:00 pm							
10:15							
10:30							
10:45							
11:00 pm							
11:15							
11:30							
11.45							

Charlie, 31, parent/freelancer

Time	Mon	Tue	Wed	Thurs	Fri	Sat	Sun
5:00 am 5:15 5:30 5:45	Wake up, shower, get ready	Wake up, shower, get ready	Wake up, shower, get ready	Wake up, shower, get ready	Wake up, shower, get ready	Wake up, shower, get ready	Wake up, shower, get ready
6:00 am 6:15 6:30 6:45 7:00 am 7:15 7:30 7:45	Breakfast together, get kids ready for school	Breakfast together, get kids ready for school	Breakfast together, get kids ready for school	Breakfast together, get kids ready for school	Breakfast together, get kids ready for school		Get kids up and ready
8:00 am 8:15 8:30 8:45	School drop off	School drop off	School drop off	School drop off	School drop off		Breakfast and catch-up at coffee shop
9:00 am 9:15 9:30 9:45	Work	Work	Work	Work	Work	Family free time	
10:00 am 10:15 10:30 10:45 11:00 am	Work	Work	Work	Work	Work		
11:15 11:30 11:45 12:00 pm 12:15							Family free time
12:30 12:45	Lunch	Lunch	Lunch	Lunch	Lunch		

Time	Mon	Tue	Wed	Thurs	Fri	Sat	Sun
1:00 pm	Work	Work	Work	Work	Work		
1:15							
1:30							
1:45							
2:00 pm							
2:15							
2:30							
2:45	School pick up	School pick up	School pick up	School pick up	School pick up		
3:00 pm							
3:15							
3:30	Family free time	Family free time	Family free time	Family free time	Family free time	Family free time	Family free time
3:45							
4:00 pm							
4:15							
4:30							
4:45							
5:00 pm		Homework		Homework			
5:15							
5:30	Homework	Driving	Homework	Driving	Homework		
5:45							
6:00 pm							
6:15		Spin class, kids at creche		Spin class, kids at creche			
6:30	Dinner		Dinner		Dinner		
6:45							
7:00 pm	Family free time	Driving	Family free time	Driving	Family free time		
7:15		Quick Dinner		Quick Dinner			
7:30							
7:45	Bedtime routine	Bedtime routine	Bedtime routine	Bedtime routine	Bedtime routine	Bedtime routine	Bedtime routine
8:00 pm							
8:15	Free time by myself	Free time by myself	Free time by myself	Free time by myself	Free time by myself	Free time by myself	Free time by myself
8:30							
8:45							
9:00 pm							
9:15							
9:30	Reading in bed	Reading in bed	Reading in bed	Reading in bed	Reading in bed	Reading in bed	Reading in bed
9:45							
10:00 pm	Sleep	Sleep	Sleep	Sleep	Sleep	Sleep	Sleep

Josh, 19, student

Our next case study is Josh, a university student. Josh used this system to sort out his calendar and his priorities.

In My Own Words

"I'm 19, and I'm in my second year of university, studying law. I scraped by with decent results last year but the workload is picking up and it's time to get organised. I've got a casual job at a café, plus I try to see my family, catch up with high school friends, and spend time with my uni friends."

Current To Do List System

"To be honest I don't really have a to do list system. I've got my uni timetable and I keep a list of upcoming tests, exams, and assignment due dates, but that's it. The roster at the café changes each week, and I don't find out until Saturday what the roster is for the following week.

My main problem is getting an early start on assignments and allowing time to study for tests and exams. Somehow I always end up leaving everything to the last minute."

Write Your Goal/Mission Statement

"To make the most of this opportunity and not throw away my education. It's not enough to scrape by and get decent results. I want to know that the marks I get represent my very best."

Work Out Your Not-Negotiables

Sleep

"I'm someone who needs my eight hours - minimum. I need to plan in advance so I get enough sleep on days when I have an early-morning class. It's okay to stay up late if I can sleep in in the morning. But I've got to stop staying up until 2:00 a.m. and then expecting to be at my best at a 9:00 a.m. lecture."

Working Hours

"My contact hours (lectures, tutorials, and labs) are set at the start of each semester. My hours at the café change each week, but it's pretty much always three evenings during the week and one weekend day."

Family and Friends

"I'm juggling separate groups for the first time, which is proving hard to navigate. I don't want to fall out of touch with my high school friends, but I also want to spend time with my new uni friends. I also need to make sure I spend decent time with my family, especially my little brothers. I know they miss me since I moved out of home."

Long-Term Goals

"I promised myself that I'd start working on some screenplays as soon as I left home and was at uni. I'm now well into my second year and I still haven't started. I know that once I finish uni and start working in law I won't have any time at all. I'll kick myself if I don't take this opportunity now."

Notes On Calendar Blocking

"My schedule changes weekly because of the café roster, and daily because of my uni timetable. This chaos plays with my head. I'd benefit if I could standardise my timetable a bit.

For example, my earliest contact hour is a 9 o'clock lecture three days a week. Even though I don't start until later in the day on the other two days, I should treat every day as if I have a 9 o'clock start. I should spend that time studying or doing assignments.

I need to treat my study as a full-time job, rather than just popping in every time I have a lecture. After all, we were warned to expect three or four hours of study for every hour of contact time.

I can do the same with my work schedule. I usually work three evenings a week from 5:00 p.m. to 8:00 p.m.

I should put it in my calendar as if I work every evening Monday to Friday. On nights when I'm not working, I can do something else, like catching up with my family. My parents and brothers would love to have me come over for dinner two nights a week. I know they wouldn't care if those nights change each week."

Time	Mon	Tue	Wed	Thurs	Fri	Sat	Sun
7:30							
7:45	Get up, breakfast, get ready, pack bag	Get up, breakfast, get ready, pack bag	Get up, breakfast, get ready, pack bag	Get up, breakfast, get ready, pack bag	Get up, breakfast, get ready, pack bag	Sleep in	Sleep in
8:00 am							
8:15							
8:30							
8:45							
9:00 am						Get ready for work (check roster)	Get ready for work (check roster)
9:15							
9:30							
9:45							
10:00 am	Uni - classes, lectures, study	Uni - classes, lectures, study	Uni - classes, lectures, study	Uni - classes, lectures, study	Uni - classes, lectures, study	Work (check roster) or study	Work (check roster) or study
10:15							
10:30							
10:45							
11:00 am							
11:15							
11:30							
11:45							
12:00 pm							
12:15							
12:30							
12:45							

Time	Mon	Tue	Wed	Thurs	Fri	Sat	Sun
1:00 pm 1:15 1:30 1:45						Work (check roster) or study	Work (check roster) or study
2:00 pm 2:15 2:30 2:45	Uni - classes, lectures, study	Uni - classes, lectures, study	Uni - classes, lectures, study	Uni - classes, lectures, study	Uni - classes, lectures, study		
3:00 pm 3:15 3:30 3:45							
4:00 pm 4:15 4:30 4:45	Go home, get ready	Go home, get ready	Go home, get ready	Go home, get ready	Go home, get ready		
5:00 pm 5:15 5:30 5:45 6:00 pm 6:15 6:30 6:45 7:00 pm 7:15 7:30 7:45	Café work (check roster) or dinner at home	Café work (check roster) or dinner at home	Café work (check roster) or dinner at home	Café work (check roster) or dinner at home	Café work (check roster) or dinner at home	Free time	Free time (bed by 10!)
8:00 pm 8:15 8:30 8:45 9:00 pm 9:15 9:30 9:45	Free time (bed by 10!)	Free time (bed by 10!)	Free time (bed by 10!)	Free time (bed by 10!)	Free time		

Review Your Current To Do List

With your not-negotiables in place, you have the basic outline of your calendar. Well done! You've finished the big picture, and now it's time to add in the details. Now you'll break down bigger blocks currently assigned to broad topics like "work".

Take out your current to do list, or pile of lists if you have more than one. If there are tasks that you do without checking them off, write them down. For example, your to do list might not include routine tasks like checking emails or texts.

If you don't currently work from a list at all, take the time now to write everything down.

On a blank sheet document, write a heading for each of the major blocks of time currently in your new calendar. We'll start with the big one - work. You can later repeat the process for other major blocks of time, like "exercise", "free time", and "family time". It may be the case that you only need to flesh out the work section. It all depends on the current to do list system you're working from.

Does your to do list include personal tasks like cooking, washing, cleaning, and bills? If so, go through these same steps for your home life after you've finished the work sections.

Let's start with your list of tasks for work. If you already have a list, that's a great start. Then add any tasks you do without being prompted, like checking your email. Ask yourself:

- What tasks do I do every day?
- How do I spend my time when I'm at work?

Be honest with yourself. It's for your own benefit, and your boss or clients will never see your list. Include tasks that you know you shouldn't spend time on but you do anyway, like:

- Checking social media
- Making personal phone calls
- Playing games on your phone.

Feeling stuck and don't know what you usually do during your working time? It could be because you run on autopilot, or because you use your email inbox as a makeshift to do list. If so, stop here and give yourself some time to create your list.

Track your work activities over the next week and write down everything you do. Don't worry about writing down every time you do the same activity. If you've already written "Check emails" the first time you do it, you don't need to note it again the next time you do it.

Before long, you'll have a list to work from. Your task now is to separate this list into two - repeating tasks and one-off tasks.

- Repeating tasks are things you do every day, or even several times a day, like checking email.
- One-off tasks include writing a report, sending a specific email, or making a phone call.

In the coming steps, you'll put your repeating tasks into your calendar. You'll no longer need a to do list for those items. Your one-off tasks will go into a separate list to help you prioritise and keep track of due dates.

But for now, keep working on your list of all the tasks you do during your working time. Then split your list into two: repeating tasks and one-off tasks.

You may notice that some of the items written down don't fall into either category:

- The name of a book your friend recommended
- A friend's birthday
- A motivational quote you liked so much you had to write it down.

We'll deal with anything that isn't either a repeating task or a one-off task in the next section.

Charlie, 31, parent/freelancer

Review Your Current To Do List

Work

Repeating Tasks

- *Check email for anything new or important*
- *Read through and delete newsletters and other generic emails*
- *Reply to business emails*
- *Reply to personal emails*
- *Check business social media accounts, reply to comments*
- *Write new social media posts*
- *Invoicing - create new invoices, check old invoices for payment, send reminders*
- *Check freelancing sites, apply for new projects*
- *Update resume and portfolio with recent projects*
- *Check job sites and tender boards for new big projects to bid on*

One-Off Tasks

- *Second round of amendments for coffee shop logo*
- *Sketch three homepage design ideas for ad agency*
- *Finalise law firm newsletter layout and submit*
- *Follow up with copywriter, source stock images for upcoming social media posts for hair salon*
- *Brief photographer before next week's boutique photo shoot*

Create Your "Notes To Self" List

Here's an uncomfortable fact about to do lists.

You will never complete a good number of the tasks you write in a traditional to do list. Not only will you not complete them, you won't start them.

Of course, people don't know that when they add the item to their list. No one would write down a task with the intention of never doing it. But the reality is that most people are too busy to:

- Watch the funny video their high school friend sent
- Read the book their relative recommended
- Or even check for cheaper prices from rival health insurance funds.

Even though you'll likely never complete these tasks, you should still write them down. Why? Because writing things down helps to get them out of your head. This frees up your valuable brainpower for more important tasks.

Picture your mind like a Ferris Wheel. Each compartment contains some little thing you're trying to remember:

- A quote you liked
- The forecast for the weekend
- A reminder to buy a birthday card
- A book idea you had in the shower.

All these little thoughts are going around and around. Writing them down gets them out of your mind, giving you an immediate feeling of peace. Finally your brain can concentrate on more important tasks - like driving - rather than churning the same thoughts.

Later, we'll talk about the benefits of having a notebook - either real or virtual - with you at all times. But for now, it's time to create a "Notes to Self" list. This list can be either real or virtual. A Word or Excel document would work well, or a cloud-based Google Doc or Sheet.

A virtual list gives you the benefit of being able to move the items around into groups:

- All birthdays together
- A list of book recommendations all in one place
- Another list of YouTube videos to watch one day
- All your favourite motivational quotes in one place.

But if you prefer to work with pen and paper, that will work just as well.

You would have a list of everything from your current to do list that is neither a repeating task nor a one-off task. This is now your "Notes to Self" list. Now you have a record of all these notes and ideas, but they're no longer competing with actual tasks.

You will likely never action most of the items on the list - and that's okay. What you will be able to do is reference it if you need to. When your friend asks, "What was the name of that book I told you about last year?", you can look it up from your list. When you're stuck on a long commute or have an hour to wait at an airport, you've got a list of YouTube videos to watch.

What's most important is that your mind is now free to concentrate on more important tasks. No longer is your mind stuck churning over the same list of things to remember.

Charlie, 31, parent/freelancer

Create Your "Notes To Self" List

- *Do a Udemy drawing course together with the kids - udemy.com/draw-cute-characters ?*
- *Mini notebook craft - https://youtu.be/Y-XcyV9rwwY*
- *Furry notebook DIY - https://www.youtube.com/watch?v=kLAdEgtgLQA*
- *"They may forget what you said, but they will never forget how you made them feel." - Carol Buchner*

Create Your Task List

Now it's time to deal with your one-off tasks.

Create a new document called your "Task List" to track and prioritise your one-off tasks.

For now we're still working within your "Work" block of time. For many people this will be the only area that requires a task list. You may find it helpful to follow these same steps again for another block of time in your calendar, like:

- Free time
- Exercise
- Study
- Working towards a particular goal.

For now, let's continue to concentrate on your "Work" space. Everything from your previous list designated a one-off task is going to go on your new task list. Start with the following headings, but remember you can tweak them as necessary in the future.

Assigned Date	Due Date	Description	Urgency /10	Importance /10	Alignment with Goals /10

Assigned Date - the date the project or task was first assigned to you. It's not the date you started work on it, but the date that responsibility for it first fell into your hands.

Due Date - the date by which you must complete the task. This may have been:

- Set by your superior or client
- Negotiated between you and the other party
- Assign by yourself, especially if this task is one element of a larger project.

Description - a short description or the title of the task, without going into too much detail.

Urgency - usually refers to someone else's priorities, rather than yours. A task designated as "urgent" is usually one that someone else wants you to complete so they can do what they need to do. Maybe they've left it to the last minute to assign the task to you, or they're impatient. Unless you're the one who left something to the last minute, urgency refers to the other party.

In this column, give this task a score out of 10 for how urgent it is. Will you have angry phone calls and emails waiting for you if you don't deliver this immediately? When we come to prioritising your tasks you'll see that urgency is one of the factors to consider.

Importance - the spotlight is now back to your priorities and your needs. From your point of view, how important is this task? The way you define important will depend on your circumstances and the type of work you do.

- A task assigned by a long-term client may be more important than a one-off client.
- A task assigned by a new client may be more important as you seek to impress them and secure future work.
- A task that tests your skills may be more important than simple busywork.

- A task assigned by a senior supervisor may be more important than a routine task.
- A task with a higher rate of pay may get a higher importance score than lower paying tasks.

Alignment with Goals - we now come back to the goal or mission statement you created earlier. A task may be both urgent and important, yet may not align with the goals you've set for yourself.

Let's take an example. You work as a freelancer performing two roles:

- Legal transcription, where you type out courtroom proceedings, and
- Copywriting, where you write articles and website copy for businesses.

Transcription pays the bills and is a steady source of income, but it's not a fulfilling job. You don't see it as your ultimate career.

You want to transition away from transcription and concentrate more on copywriting. When setting your goals earlier in the book, you stated that your goals are to:

- Build up your copywriting business
- Take on more high-paying copywriting clients
- Reduce your transcription workload as you increase your copywriting work.

You're now assigned a new transcription task. Your client stresses the urgency of the task, and is offering a high rate of pay. That earns it high marks in both urgency and importance. But the task doesn't align with the goals you set for yourself. That's why it should receive a lower score in the Alignment with Goals column.

Go ahead and fill in the table with your list of one-off tasks. Enter the items in any order for now. In the next step, we'll go through prioritising your list.

Charlie, 31, parent/freelancer

Create Your Task List

Assigned Date	Due Date	Description	Urgency /10	Importance /10	Alignment with Goals /10
29 Jan	-	Second round of amendments for coffee shop logo	1	1	10
26 Jan	1 Mar	Sketch three homepage design ideas for ad agency	1	9	5
28 Jan	5 Feb	Finalise law firm newsletter layout and submit	8	9	5
15 Jan	3 Feb	Follow up with copywriter, source stock images for upcoming social media posts for hair salon	6	4	2
15 Jan	3 Feb	Brief photographer before next week's boutique photoshoot	9	5	5

Prioritise Your Task List

The next step is to prioritise your task list. This is where you'll list your tasks in the order that you intend to complete them. Then you can work through the list from top to bottom.

The value of a properly ordered task list is enormous. By prioritising your task list considering several variables, you're almost guaranteeing your success. Why? Many people spend considerable time each day deciding what to work on next. This is often followed by feelings of guilt or panic from making the wrong decision.

Has this ever happened to you? You spend all week working on a task, then realise you've forgotten about another one? The second task now has an impossibly short deadline.

By prioritising your tasks in advance, you can remove the daily decision-making process. Instead, you can get to work, knocking off the tasks one at a time in the order that you've placed them on your list.

Productivity experts tend to talk about your Most Important Task (or MIT). The theory is that, if you always know your MIT, you can concentrate on it to the exclusion of less important tasks. By preparing your task list in this way, you'll always know your MIT. Better yet, once you've finished your MIT, the second task on your list takes top priority and becomes your new MIT.

How, then, do you prioritise your tasks? Your first consideration must always be the due date column. Submitting work late or failing to deliver on promises made is an enormous no-no. You may get away with a late submission on a rare occasion. You could even ask for an extension under special circumstances, but doing so regularly will damage your reputation and cause your clients or supervisor to look elsewhere.

A task may have scores for importance and alignment with goals, but if it's assigned to you, you must complete it - and before the due date.

Your first step is to put your tasks in order by their due date.

If you're working in a computer document, reordering your list is as simple as cutting and pasting. If you prefer to work with pen and paper, number each item, with 1 representing the top of the list. Once you've finished prioritising your list, rewrite it in the correct order.

If a task does not have a due date, it's a good idea to create a draft due date for yourself.

- Is the task a smaller part of a larger or ongoing project? Assign a due date that gives you plenty of time to move on to the next phase of the project.
- Has someone assigned you a task without a due date? Estimate a due date based on when you think your client or supervisor will follow up with you about the task.

Write estimated due dates in brackets so they aren't confused with official due dates.

Charlie, 31, parent/freelancer

Prioritise Your Task List

Ordering Tasks by Due Date

Assigned Date	Due Date	Description	Urgency /10	Importance /10	Alignment with Goals /10
15 Jan	3 Feb	Follow up with copywriter, source stock images for upcoming social media posts for hair salon	6	4	2
15 Jan	3 Feb	Brief photographer before next week's boutique photoshoot	9	5	5
28 Jan	5 Feb	Finalise law firm newsletter layout and submit	8	9	5
29 Jan	(15 Feb)	Second round of amendments for coffee shop logo	1	1	10
26 Jan	1 Mar	Sketch three homepage design ideas for ad agency	1	9	5

Now it's time to look at the last three columns - urgency, importance, and alignment with goals. There is no set formula for ranking tasks based on these three columns; however, by having three separate scores to work with, you can ensure you're not:

- confusing urgency with importance, or
- prioritising tasks that don't align with your ultimate goals over ones that do.

Once you've got your task list finalised, leave it to one side for the moment. We'll be coming back to this list again very soon.

Charlie, 31, parent/freelancer

Ordering Tasks by Priority

"After ordering the tasks by due date, I realised that I had two tasks due in two days' time that I had been ignoring. Both of these involved simple tasks like emails and an internet search. I could have them done in less than 30 minutes each. Yet I'd been putting them off for more than two weeks!

These are the tasks that would see me waking up in a panic, realising I'd left something to the last minute again. It's eye opening seeing the tasks listed by due date. It will be so simple to knock off the first two tasks from my list with about an hour's work. I'll keep those two tasks at the top of my new prioritised task list."

Assigned Date	Due Date	Description	Urgency /10	Importance /10	Alignment with Goals /10
15 Jan	3 Feb	Follow up with copywriter, source stock images for upcoming social media posts for hair salon	6	4	2
15 Jan	3 Feb	Brief photographer before next week's boutique photoshoot	9	5	5

"I've now got three tasks left to put in order.

- *One is due in five days' time.*
- *The next has no due date but I've estimated that the client will start following up with me around mid-February.*
- *The last one isn't due for another month.*

I'm now looking at the urgency and importance columns. I've noted that the law firm is pretty insistent that I make their work a priority. I guess that's how some law firms work - they know how to keep people on their toes.

I also want to consider how these tasks align with my goals.

Despite the law firm's insistence on their work being urgent, it scores a 5 for alignment with goals. My goal is to move away from that type of graphic design work and concentrate on logo design and creation.

The second round of amendments for the coffee shop's logo has no due date. The owner of the coffee shop is very polite and laid-back, and isn't as demanding as other clients. But this logo work is exactly the type of work I want to be doing more of, so I've scored it 10 for alignment with goals. The client has already said I can use the finalised logo - along with some of the design ideas - in my portfolio. I'm going to tackle this task next."

Assigned Date	Due Date	Description	Urgency /10	Importance /10	Alignment with Goals /10
15 Jan	3 Feb	Follow up with copywriter, source stock images for upcoming social media posts for hair salon	6	4	2
15 Jan	3 Feb	Brief photographer before next week's boutique photoshoot	9	5	5
29 Jan	(15 Feb)	Second round of amendments for coffee shop logo	1	1	10

"The two remaining tasks both scored a 5 for alignment with goals column, but one is due before the other. I'll tackle them in that order."

Assigned Date	Due Date	Description	Urgency /10	Importance /10	Alignment with Goals /10
15 Jan	3 Feb	Follow up with copywriter, source stock images for upcoming social media posts for hair salon	6	4	2
15 Jan	3 Feb	Brief photographer before next week's boutique photoshoot	9	5	5
29 Jan	(15 Feb)	Second round of amendments for coffee shop logo	1	1	10
28 Jan	5 Feb	Finalise law firm newsletter layout and submit	8	9	5
26 Jan	1 Mar	Sketch three homepage design ideas for ad agency	1	9	5

Batch Your Repeating Tasks

It's time to take out the list of repeating tasks you created earlier. The aim of this section is to:

- Group your tasks in a logical way
- Schedule them in your calendar so you can tackle a bunch of similar tasks in one go.

If you're like most people, you're guilty of doing the same task several times a day without even realising it. Not sure if this applies to you? Make a note of how many times each day you check your phone or check your emails.

Many people do these tasks without even realising they're doing it. For some people, it's classic FOMO - the fear of missing out on a new email or being out of the loop on something. For others, it's a sign of boredom or a way to procrastinate from tackling more important tasks. Whatever the reason, it's destroying your productivity and eating into your working time. And it's happening more than you even realise.

You may have your emails set up to notify you when a new message hits your inbox. If you leave your desk you're checking for new messages on your phone, then again on your computer once you return to your desk.

It's time to take back control and put some limits on this habit. It will feel strange at first, and you'll worry about missing something important. Remember that most people don't expect an immediate reply to an email. A reply within 24 hours, yes, but not a reply so immediate that you have to check your phone several times a minute. If you were in a meeting or on a flight you wouldn't be able to check your emails. Nothing bad is going to happen for those few hours.

Look through your list of repeating tasks and note any items that relate to emails. For example:

- Check business email
- Check personal email
- Sort out your inbox
- Reply to the most important emails
- Read through newsletters and other FYI type emails

You're going to batch all these tasks together.

Next, go into the settings of your computer and phone and turn off email notifications. It's fine to still have your email account set up on your phone, but you need to disable the familiar "ding" and the preview pop-up every time a new message arrives. These distractions pull your attention and destroy your concentration and focus.

You now have a new repeating task - "Emails" - which batches several tasks on your list. In the next step, you'll choose the exact times to perform this task. For emails, it makes sense to schedule it for two or three times a day, depending on your circumstances. Outside of those times, you'll be concentrating on other tasks and won't check your emails. This new habit will sting at first and it will take practice, but once you see how your productivity soars as a result you won't want to go back to your old ways.

Here's another point to consider about immediately replying to emails. When you do so, you cause others to feel that they too need to action emails immediately. This is especially the case if you are their superior.

Think about it from their point of view. Imagine your boss sending you a barrage of emails every day. Imagine how difficult it would be to concentrate on an assigned task. Feeling guilty about ignoring your boss's emails, you'd prioritise replying - even if it meant delaying your actual work. Waiting until your next email session gives other people a break from their own inboxes.

Have a look at the other items on your repeating tasks list and see how you can batch them together. This will of course depend on the type of work you do and other individual circumstances. Examples include:

- Returning phone calls, including checking voice messages
- Set office hours when your staff or co-workers know you're available
- Financial, including checking bank accounts, and paying invoices
- Invoicing, including creating new invoices and following up outstanding invoices
- Social media, including creating new posts and replying to comments and messages

- Applying for new projects and creating quotes.

Charlie, 31, parent/freelancer

Batch Your Repeating Tasks

Repeating Tasks

Emails

- *Check email for anything new or important*
- *Read through and delete newsletters and other generic emails*
- *Reply to business emails*
- *Reply to personal emails*

Social Media

- *Check business social media accounts, reply to comments*
- *Write new social media posts*

Invoicing

- *Invoicing - create new invoices, check for payment of old invoices, send reminders*

New Work

- *Check freelancing sites, apply for new projects*
- *Update resume and portfolio with recent projects*
- *Check job sites and tender boards for new projects*

It's almost time to start slotting your new list of tasks into your calendar. But before you do so, there are a few concepts you need to understand first.

Essential Skill to Master: Understanding When You Are Most Productive
When are you most productive?

- Do you hit the ground running and get your best work done as soon as you arrive at the office?
- Does it take you a while to warm up, and you don't hit your stride until after you've had your mid-morning coffee?
- Is it towards the end of the day when everything starts fitting together and you're doing your best work?

Understanding when in your day you feel the most alert, awake, and ready to achieve is essential. This requires introspection and reviewing your mood and energy throughout the day. If you're not sure, track yourself over the next few working days.

Mood and energy can be hard to gauge, especially when looking back. Rather than assessing your mood at the end of the day, try this simple experiment. Every hour on the hour, give yourself a score out of 10 in three areas - mood, focus, and energy. Doing so will take less than 30 seconds and will give you valuable insights into your hourly productivity.

Armed with this information, you can block time in your calendar in a way that makes sense for you.

Charlie, 31, parent/freelancer

Essential Skill to Master: Understanding When You Are Most Productive

"It definitely takes me a while to get going when I start work. I've already spent hours getting the kids up and ready for school, and have done the first of two school runs for the day. I'm ready for a break by then! I often check emails or mess around on social media rather than get started on work. This has the knock-on effect of a good dose of guilt to start my working day.

I once read that if you lose an hour in the morning you'll spend the rest of the day trying to catch it. That's me most days.

Knowing what I know now, I'm going to schedule an easier task first thing in the morning. I'll have the satisfaction of getting something done and sticking with the plan. But it's not the right time for me to dive into difficult projects first thing."

Essential Skill to Master: Understanding What Motivates You

What motivates you? A typical answer might be:

- A promotion or pay rise
- Providing for your family
- Working towards an early retirement.

Those are all worthy goals, but this question is a little different.

- When you're working on a task that you'd rather not be doing, what is it that makes you continue working?
- What thoughts run through your mind?
- What stops you from taking the easy route and having a break or doing something else?

Imagine you're working on a task that is boring, tedious or otherwise interesting. You have to do it, but you'd rather do anything else.

Knowing how to motivate yourself to get through unpleasant tasks is vital. This knowledge can define an effective calendar system.

The following statements represent very different mindsets. Each one is motivating to some people yet completely counter-productive to others. Do any of those resonate with you?

I get through this task by thinking of a way that I can reward myself later.

Example: "If I can complete this task today, I'll make an appointment for a massage on the weekend." "If I can complete this task by lunchtime, I'll go to my favourite café for lunch and save my bagged lunch for tomorrow."

How to use this information: Make a list of all the ways that you can reward yourself for completing tasks. Add to your list as you think of new potential rewards.

Try to keep each one simple, inexpensive, and easy to access. A trip to Bali would be lovely, but you're unlikely to book one for finishing a report on time.

Remember to follow through. Make the massage appointment, book the movie tickets, or head out for lunch as soon as the task is over.

I get through this task because I can do something easier or more rewarding straight afterwards.

Example: "After I finish this report, I'll do something easier like replying to some emails." "I've been looking forward to scheduling next week's social media posts. I'll spend the morning getting this harder task out of the way before doing the social media work."

How to use this information: Sprinkle easier or interesting tasks between more difficult tasks. Don't plan to work for a full day on a difficult task. Set up your calendar to spend a block of time working on the task, followed by a shorter, easier task. Repeat the same schedule so you always have an easier task to look forward to after a block of hard work.

I get through this task because I told someone I would, and I don't want to feel ashamed or that I've let them down.

Example: "I told everyone at the planning meeting on Monday that I'd have this done by Wednesday at the latest. I'd be so embarrassed if I don't meet this deadline." "I told my mentors that I was giving myself all day today to finish this task. If I don't have it done, they'll think I was goofing off all day."

How to use this information: If you're motivated by external accountability, use this to your advantage. Find a mentor or accountability buddy to report to. It may take some time and a few false starts before you find the right person, but the effort will be worth it once you have a good accountability relationship set up.

You're looking for someone with a unique mix of qualities:

- Knowledge and experience in your area so that they understand your various tasks
- A level of seniority or power so you don't want to let them down
- Interest in you and time to spare so that they don't forget to follow up and keep you accountable.

Once you've found the right mentor or accountability buddy:

- Stay in contact
- Give them a copy of your calendar
- Be honest about your workload and time limitations
- Keep them updated on your projects and deadlines
- Allow them to help keep you motivated.

I get through this task because I know there is a strict time limit and the deadline is looming.

Example: "This is due in 30 minutes, and I must have it done. I can see my boss walking around the office, and I know they'll be following up if this isn't done on time." "When I've got all day to work on one task, I struggle to get anything done. But when that same task is due in 30 minutes, I get all fired up and would move mountains to get it done on time."

How to use this information: If you work best with a deadline hanging over your head, make the most of this information. Create artificial deadlines to work towards. You know you'll lack motivation if something isn't due for another two weeks. Give yourself a much shorter deadline and stick to it.

Tell the client exactly when the work will be ready, or recruit an accountability buddy to hold you to it. Make sure they're ready to follow up when the task is due to keep you on your toes.

I get through this task because I like to measure my progress and see if I can beat yesterday.

Example: "I submitted $X of client work yesterday, and I'm going to see if I can beat that total today." "Yesterday my productivity rate at work was 81%, and today I'm determined to beat it."

How to use this information: What gets measured gets improved. If you measure your productivity, maintaining this habit can keep you motivated. This can include measuring:

- Money earned
- Hours spent working
- Productivity percentage (minutes working as a proportion of the total working time).

A simple spreadsheet and graph combination allow you to visually track your progress.

- If you're a freelancer or have a variable income, try recording the amount of money you earn each day. You won't want to want to ruin your graph with a significant dip on one day because you felt unmotivated.

- If you're a student or have a fixed salary, try recording the amount of time you spend studying or working each day.
- If you have set working hours, record your productivity percentage. For example, assume you have five hours to work (300 minutes). You make coffee, chat to colleagues, browse social media, and only manage 60 minutes of work. You're productivity percentage is 20% for the day. Record this on a chart and try to beat it tomorrow. A simple stopwatch app on your phone or computer will record your time worked.

Another method is to divide your working time into 15-minute intervals. Then, measure your output for each segment. This method works well with tasks that are easily measured.

For example, you're working on a report or assignment. Note your word count every 15 minutes and calculate how many words you produced each segment.

Not only does this method help to keep track of your productivity over time, it offers another bonus. Measuring every 15 minutes helps to avoid the temptation to do something else for "just a few minutes". We all know that those few minutes will stretch out to a much longer period. This will become clear when you see that you produced zero words in the last 15 minutes.

I get through this task because I've thought of a punishment for myself if I don't.

Example: "If this task isn't finished by the end of today, I'm giving away my basketball season tickets." "I've got $50 cash in a sealed envelope and I've given it to my colleague. They have strict instructions to post it to a charity I hate unless I can prove I've finished this task today."

How to use this information: Motivation by punishment is not for the faint of heart. But if the thought of

- donating money to your least favourite charity
- giving away something of value to you, or
- missing out on an experience you would have enjoyed

keep the fires of motivation burning, use this knowledge to your advantage. The trick is to follow through if you don't achieve what you set out to do. If you know that the punishment isn't really going to happen, the trick loses its effect.

Set up your punishment in advance. Put cash or something else you value in a sealed envelope and hand it to someone you trust. They're only to give it back if you can prove that you completed the task. Don't choose someone who will take pity on you or accept your excuses for not having completed the task. Choose someone who will hold you to your word.

Charlie, 31, parent/freelancer

Essential Skill to Master: Understanding What Motivates You

"I'm motivated by rewards, and there were two items on the list that resonated with me. First, I'm motivated by rewards I can give myself for completing something on time. I love treating the kids to something fun after school instead of coming straight home. A reward could be that I take the kids to a water park, play centre, or to go out for a snack after school.

Second, I'm motivated by knowing I've got an easier task coming up. With this in mind, I'll break up bigger tasks with easier work like emails."

Optional Skill to Master: Estimating Time

The ability to estimate the time a particular task will take is a useful skill to have. The calendar system doesn't rely on time estimates, making this an optional skill. But honing your time estimating skills can benefit you in several ways.

- If a task doesn't have a due date, the ability to estimate how long the task will take can help you to set a realistic due date.
- If your job involves quoting for projects, proper time estimating is crucial. Underestimating the time a project will take could cause you to undercut yourself. You'll then feel frustrated as the project blows out and takes more time than you allowed. Overestimating time causes high quotes and lost projects or clients.

When prioritising your task list, the amount of time to complete a project is a relevant consideration. You may even choose to add a time estimation column to your task list.

Estimating time is a skill, and - like all other skills - you can improve with practice and repetition. If you find that you struggle with time estimations, start now to hone your skills. Before you complete any task - whether at work or at home - write down how long you think the task will take. Time yourself as you complete the task and compare the results.

Most people tend to underestimate the amount of time it takes to complete tasks. You will know what your tendency is once you start tracking yourself.

Repeat this process as much as possible. You'll soon find that you make more accurate time estimates.

Blocking Time In Your Calendar

Now it's time to go back to your calendar and block in these new tasks you've identified in the previous steps. Remember that we're still focusing on the "Work" block of time. Concentrate on this area and ignore the rest of your calendar for now.

At this point you are now armed with an incredible amount of information. You are aware of when you are most productive, and you know the tricks to keep yourself motivated.

Your Last Appointment Every Day Is A Review

The first thing to do is set aside the last 15 minutes of every working day for a review. We'll come to what will happen during your daily review later. For now, make sure it's sitting there as the last 15 minutes of every working day.

Blocking Time To Work On Your Task List

The next step is to decide the proportion of your time to spend working through your task list. For most people, the items in your task list are your bread and butter.

- If you're self-employed or a freelancer, these are the projects you can invoice for.
- If you're an employee, these are the tasks that will impress your employer and win you a promotion.
- If you're a student, these are the assignments and study sessions that will impact your grade.

Repeating tasks are those that - although necessary - don't impact your success. For example, imagine you're a freelancer. Applying for new projects is an essential item for you to complete, and is on your repeating task list. But time spent applying for new projects remains an unbillable task. Spending an hour actually completing projects for your existing clients is billable. Unless you keep bringing in new work, you'll soon fail as a freelancer. But it's also important not to spend a disproportionate amount of time doing so.

If you're not sure what proportion of your working day to devote to your task list, start with around two thirds. In other words, spend two hours working through your task list for every hour of repeating tasks. These time allocations include short breaks, so you can't expect 100% productivity.

Your calendar will always be a work in progress, and you can adjust your times as needed.

Now that you know how many hours per day to dedicate to your task list, it's time to schedule this in your calendar. Remember your insights about when you're most productive and what motivates you. Use this knowledge to schedule your "task list" time.

Let's take an example. In the previous steps you determined:

- You're most productive first thing in the morning, and
- You're motivated by being accountable to someone else.

Schedule your task list time at the start of the day. Begin every day by checking in with your mentor or accountability buddy, then get to work. Schedule your repeating tasks for later in the day. By then, you'll have expended some of your energy and motivation on your morning task list work.

Charlie, 31, parent/freelancer

Blocking Time In Your Calendar

Blocking Time To Work On Your Task List

"I get five hours to work each school day, from 9:00 a.m. until 2:45 p.m., allowing for 30 minutes for lunch. I'll aim for three hours for my task list and

two hours for repeating tasks. Knowing what I know now about my productivity, I doubt I've ever done three hours of billable work before!

I now understand that I can't expect to jump straight into my task list when I first get to work. I need to start with something easier as I come down from my hectic morning and settle into work mode. I'll leave the first 30 minutes free for a repeating task, and start work on my task list at 10:00 a.m. I'll schedule two hours of work to take me to 12 noon, then I'll do something easier for half an hour before lunch. I'll then have another hour for my task list, then 30 minutes for an easier task before I finish for the day."

9:00 am					
9:15					
9:30					
9:45					
10:00 am					
10:15					
10:30					
10:45	Task List	Task List	Task List	Task List	Task List
11:00 am					
11:15					
11:30					
11:45					
12:00 pm					
12:15					
12:30	Lunch	Lunch	Lunch	Lunch	Lunch
12:45					
1:00 pm					
1:15	Task List	Task List	Task List	Task List	Task List
1:30					
1:45					
2:00 pm					
2:15					
2:30	Review	Review	Review	Review	Review

The remaining time in your calendar is for your repeating tasks. You'll schedule some tasks a few times a week, some every day, and some - such as emails - multiple times a day. Go through your list of repeating tasks and decide how often you should tackle this task to help you stay on top of it.

Remember the aim is not to completely finish each task within each allocated session. If you schedule 30 minutes for emails in the morning, you can't expect to clear your inbox in that time. It will be enough time to:

- Review the items in your inbox
- Reply to anything urgent or important
- Send emails as necessary
- Continue actioning older emails.

Working to a time limit, rather than insisting on finishing each task, keeps you moving.

At the start of this book we discussed the concept that your to do list will never be complete. That's why the calendar system works. Never again will you spend all day on emails, then feel guilty and frustrated that you didn't get any real work done. Your time limits allow you to do as much as you can within the allocated time, before moving on to another task.

Additionally, it's important to allow a small buffer of time between tasks. With your calendar divided into 15-minute intervals, you have two options:

- Leave a 15-minute gap (denoted with a grey filled in cell) between tasks, or
- Allow at least 30 minutes per task, which includes a short break.

Your aim is to start each task exactly on time. Imagine your calendar says that you're to return phone calls at 9:00 a.m. and start work on your task list at 10:00 a.m. You need to finish returning calls with enough time for a short break before starting your task list at 10:00 a.m.

It will take some juggling to fit your repeating tasks into the remaining time blocks. You may find that some parts of your day will be the same, while other tasks will change each day.

Remember that your calendar will always be a work in progress. If something isn't working, rearrange your calendar, try it out, and make further changes if necessary.

Charlie, 31, parent/freelancer

Blocking Time To Work On Your Repeating Tasks

- *Emails - twice a day*
- *Social media - a few times a week, not necessarily everyday*
- *Invoicing - twice a week*
- *New work - at least a few times a week, up to once a day*

9:00 am 9:15	Emails	Emails	Emails	Emails	Emails
9:30 9:45	New Work	New Work	New Work	New Work	New Work
10:00 am 10:15 10:30 10:45 11:00 am 11:15 11:30 11:45	Task List	Task List	Task List	Task List	Task List
12:00 pm 12:15	Social Media	Invoicing	Social Media	Invoicing	Social Media
12:30 12:45	Lunch	Lunch	Lunch	Lunch	Lunch
1:00 pm 1:15 1:30 1:45	Task List	Task List	Task List	Task List	Task List
2:00 pm 2:15	Emails	Emails	Emails	Emails	Emails
2:30	Review	Review	Review	Review	Review

Daily Steps

Congratulations! You have now transitioned from your previous to do list system to your new calendar system. You've done all the hard work. From here it's a matter of:

- Using your new system
- Tweaking and updating it as necessary
- Undertaking quick daily tasks to keep your system ticking along.

The following are the daily tasks to perform to stay on top of your new calendar system.

Carry A Notebook (Real Or Virtual) At All Times

You now know the benefits of writing things down rather than remembering a list of ideas. One of the most common traits of successful people is that they always carry a notebook. Whether physical or digital, they always have something on hand to write down notes and ideas.

In your notebook you can write any new information you receive or an idea that springs to mind, like:

- A telephone number or address
- A birthday to add to your calendar
- An idea that popped into your mind
- A short email you need to write
- An interesting point to do an online search for
- A quick task you need to take care of.

As you now know, the calendar system runs on the idea that tasks only occur in their designated time. It is no longer permissible to interrupt your work to answer the phone or check your emails.

But there is one exception to this rule. It is always permissible to write down something that occurs to you in your notebook at any time.

Doing so will not break your concentration. In fact, your concentration was already broken by the appearance of the thought in your mind. Writing it down:

- Takes the thought out of your mind
- Allows you to recommence concentrating on the task at hand

- Frees up the section of your brain that would have churned over the same idea for fear of losing it.

As soon as the thought pops into your head, stop immediately to write in your notebook. Then turn back to what you were working on. Don't stop to actually perform the task – just stop to write it down. That gets it out of your head and allows you to return your focus to where it was.

What happens to the things you write in your notebook? This happens during the daily review. The options are:

- New one-off tasks will go on your task list
- New repeating tasks will join an existing task batch or will form a new one
- Items that don't need immediate action go on your notes-to-self list.

Your Daily Review

In a previous step you allocated the last 15 minutes of every working day for your review. Let's discuss the aim of your daily review and some of the tasks you would perform each day during your review. 15 minutes is not a long time, and your review is not intended to be a long drawn out process. Here are some of the tasks to undertake during your review.

Look over your day's calendar and assess how well it worked for you.

- Did you follow the calendar?
- Did you run into any problems along the way?
- If you did run into problems, were they one-off problems that you couldn't help (see the FAQ section)?
- Or were they problems related to the calendar itself? For example, does a repeating task appear too often and you're running out of things to do? Or are you struggling to stay on top of a task and feel you need more time?
- Make changes to your calendar to take into account any difficulties you encountered.

Print off tomorrow's calendar

Many people find it very helpful to have a printed-out copy of each day's calendar. They find it helpful to physically tick off the blocks of time as they go. If this method works for you, print off tomorrow's calendar during your daily review.

Process any new items that came up today

- If new one-off items have come up today, add this task to your task list. Review your current task list and insert the new task in the appropriate place. Take into account its due date, urgency, importance, and alignment with your goals.
- Transfer any new item from your notepad to your task list, notes-to-self list, or repeating tasks list. If you use a physical notebook, cross off each item once you've dealt with it. If you use a digital notebook, strike through the item rather than deleting it. This way, you'll always have a record of everything from your notebook in case you want to refer to it later.

Dealing with New Items

Let's stop here for another reminder of two essential concepts.

- Your to do list will never be complete.
- You'll sometimes add new items to your list faster than you check off old items.

When a new item comes your way, there are several places it could go. Ask yourself the following questions to determine the best spot for your new item.

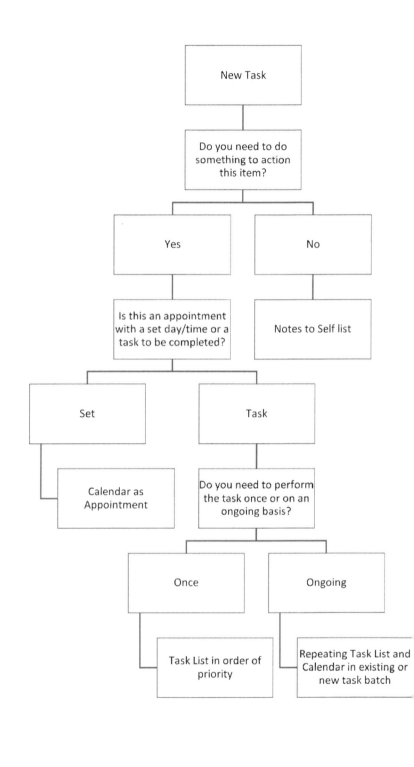

FAQs

How do I stop myself checking emails throughout the day?

The first step is to turn off automatic email notifications on all your devices. Ask yourself, what happens when you receive a new email? Does your phone vibrate or make a noise? Does a preview of the email appear on your phone's screen? Your computer may show a preview of the email in a pop-up.

This all needs to stop. These instant distractions break your concentration and pull you away from your work. Turn off automatic notifications on all your devices. Then, close out of your email program until it's time to work on emails again.

What I do when the phone rings?

The strict answer is that you don't answer your phone except during your allocated times. If you spend all day answering your phone you'll never get any of your own tasks done. In reality, though, you'd want to know who's calling. What if it's your boss? What if there is an emergency at home or with a family member?

The trick is to set yourself up for success in advance.

- Tell people when they can contact you. You've already allocated time for phone calls. Let everyone know that this is when they can call you, or when you'll return their call.
- Set up a new voicemail message that tells people when your phone hours are or when you will call them back. In the voicemail recording, encourage people to send you a text message instead.
- Buy a cheap device with a new SIM card. Guard that number like your bank details. It's only for emergencies, so give it to your child's school, your partner, and your parents. Then turn off or put away your normal device while you're working.
- Choose a different ring tone for different people so you know which calls to answer and which can wait.

What about when someone else schedules a meeting for me?

On the road to success and productivity, meetings are a roadblock. The way you'll handle meetings will depend on your role and the level of control you have over your own schedule.

- If you're in charge, block out time for meetings. Let everyone know that these are the times they can arrange to meet with you in person. Only attend meetings with a set agenda, goal, and time limit. Everyone will need to fit around you and your schedule if they want to meet with you.
- Not everyone has this level of control in their workplace. You may need to fit around existing meeting times or your boss's schedule, for example. In this case, be flexible and shuffle the other items in your calendar to accommodate the meeting.

What happens when life gets in the way?

You're sick, your child is sick, or you have to travel at the last minute. Life is always going to throw obstacles in your way. It's unrealistic to expect to follow your calendar every single day.

You'll need a degree of flexibility to shuffle your blocks of time around. If you know the interruption is coming, use your daily review to amend tomorrow's calendar.

For example, imagine you know you'll be unavailable tomorrow afternoon. Shuffle tomorrow's calendar to work on the most important tasks in the morning.

Documents

Going forward, these are the documents you'll need. This is a summary of the documents detailed in the steps above.

Daily calendar in 15-minute intervals. This can be a digital calendar or a paper version. Most people who have transitioned to the calendar system prefer a digital calendar. Digital calendars allow for automatic rolling over of repeating tasks and recurring appointments. Print out the next day's calendar during your daily review so you can cross off the items as you go.

Task list. This is your list of one-off projects in strict priority order. You've already made all the hard decisions - now you can work through the list from top to bottom.

Repeating task list. Strictly speaking, you don't need this list anymore. You've already batched and scheduled its contents into your calendar. But it can be helpful to keep a copy of your repeating task list handy. It will serve as a reminder of the tasks that make up each large block. It will also assist when adding new tasks to an existing batch.

Notes to self. This is your ongoing list of ideas, notes, links, and everything else that needs to get out of your head. You now understand that you may never action many of these items. The importance of the list is that it frees your mind to concentrate on more important tasks.

CEO Case Study
Patrick*, 43, CEO

The CEO of a household name company, who wished to remain anonymous, worked through the steps in this book.

"I honestly don't know how I got to where I am without having a proper organisational system in place. I guess it comes down to having excellent support staff who keep me on track. I rely on others to remind me where I need to be and what I should be doing".

Patrick agreed to follow the steps to move from a haphazard to do list to a streamlined calendar system. While he agreed to include his new calendar system in this book, he decided to keep his task list and notes-to-self documents private.

If you've ever wondered what the calendar of a CEO looks like, here's the final draft. You'll notice that Patrick decided not to include weekends in his calendar. He said, "I usually spend three or four hours a day working on both Saturday and Sunday. But I don't keep specific hours, and I don't make myself available for phone calls or meetings. That's family time. I only work when everyone else is occupied - usually first thing in the morning or late at night if I can't get to sleep. It just happens naturally. I'm not a TV watcher so I turn to work when other people have their downtime."

Time	Mon	Tue	Wed	Thurs	Fri
5:00 am	Wake up	Wake up	Wake up	Wake up	Wake up
5:15 / 5:30	Meditate	Meditate	Meditate	Meditate	Meditate
5:45 / 6:00 am	Breakfast, newspaper	Breakfast, newspaper	Breakfast, newspaper	Breakfast, newspaper	Breakfast, newspaper
6:15 / 6:30 / 6:45 / 7:00 am	Yoga, cardio, resistance (alternating)	Yoga, cardio, resistance (alternating)	Yoga, cardio, resistance (alternating)	Yoga, cardio, resistance (alternating)	Yoga, cardio, resistance (alternating)
7:15 / 7:30	Shower, groom	Shower, groom	Shower, groom	Shower, groom	Shower, groom
7:45 / 8:00 am / 8:15	Commute, audiobooks	Commute, audiobooks	Commute, audiobooks	Commute, audiobooks	Commute, audiobooks
8:30 / 8:45	Settle, coffee, email	Settle, coffee, email	Settle, coffee, email	Settle, coffee, email	Settle, coffee, email
9:00 am	Exec assistant	Exec assistant	Exec assistant	Exec assistant	Exec assistant
9:15 / 9:30 / 9:45	Meeting (global)	Meeting (strategy)	Meeting (sales)	Meeting (leadership)	Meeting (process)
10:00 am	Buffer	Buffer	Buffer	Buffer	Buffer
10:15 / 10:30 / 10:45	Meeting (global)	Meeting (strategy)	Meeting (sales)	Meeting (leadership)	Meeting (process)
11:00 am	Buffer	Buffer	Buffer	Buffer	Buffer
11:15 / 11:30 / 11:45	Meeting (global)	Meeting (strategy)	Meeting (sales)	Meeting (leadership)	Meeting (process)
12:00 pm / 12:15 / 12:30 / 12:45	Lunch / meeting	Lunch / meeting	Lunch / meeting	Lunch / meeting	Lunch / meeting

Time	Mon	Tue	Wed	Thurs	Fri
1:00 pm 1:15 1:30 1:45	Email	Email	Email	Email	Email
2:00 pm 2:15 2:30 2:45 3:00 pm 3:15 3:30 3:45 4:00 pm 4:15	Task list	Task list	Task list	Task list	Task list
4:30 4:45	Email	Email	Email	Email	Email
5:00 pm 5:15 5:30	Commute	Commute	Commute	Commute	Commute
5:45 6:00 pm 6:15 6:30 6:45 7:00 pm 7:15 7:30 7:45 8:00 pm 8:15 8:30 8:45	Family	Family	Family	Family	Family
9:00 pm	Bed	Bed	Bed	Bed	Bed

Here's what Patrick had to say about his calendar and daily schedule.

"I've learned to live by my calendar rather than relying on others to keep me on track. I still meet with my executive assistant every morning at 9:00 a.m. (some habits die hard!) but now it's more of a check-in and update rather than finding out my schedule for the first time.

Of course, sometimes I'm travelling and much of my daily schedule goes out the window. I still try to start the day with meditation and some kind of exercise, though. I've come to rely on both of those practices to get my day started right, but when I'm travelling I can get thrown off track by time differences, morning meetings, and other people's schedules. These days, I limit my travel as much as I can and try to encourage people to come to me.

I was introduced to meditation in the same way many people are - full of scepticism and convinced it would be a waste of my time. How wrong I was. I can't imagine starting a work-day without taking that time to be still and be present. It's changed my life.

Everyone knows I have lunch at 12. My exec assistant has a list of people (whether written down or mental, I don't know) who can schedule a lunch meeting with me if they're in town. But it can't be just anyone. That time is sacred, and I'd rather spend it alone - which I usually do two or three days a week - than suffer through a sales pitch. Lunch meetings are more social than business. It's got to be enjoyable.

Mornings are for meetings, and each day has a theme. Meetings don't start without a written agenda. I have strict time limits on my meetings. Everyone knows they start at quarter past the hour, and they don't go longer than 45 minutes. I need that 15-minute buffer to stay in control of my day. Sometimes I'll have a personal break, something to eat, or make a personal phone call. Some days I'll walk through the office and check in with people.

I schedule my meeting topics in advance, but the people I meet with changes from week to week. For example, Monday is for the global teams. I allow three meeting times for global, but it's up to my exec assistant to schedule those meetings. One week I'll have three calls with teams in Asia, and the next week might be an in-person with a visiting rep and calls to Europe. My assistant ensures I connect with all global teams on a three-week rotation.

It's the same with strategy, sales, leadership, and process. The meeting times are there, but the attendees and agendas will change. Themed days help me isolate issues and focus my attention on the needs of the distinct area of the business.

I used to have themed study days back in high school too - Mondays was English, Tuesday geography...

I tend to disappear a bit in the afternoons. I need that time to focus and concentrate. I check emails first, then turn everything off and focus. My team understands that I am visible in the morning but behind a closed door in the afternoons.

My exec assistant used to do it, but now I maintain a list (task list) of everything I'm working on.

I'm strict with myself about leaving the office at 5 o'clock. When I first started it was all the rage to burn the candle at both ends. After a few years of burnout you realise that there's only so much you can do in a day. Knowing that I could stay in the office until midnight gave me a terrible freedom. I filled the time with useless meetings and spent hours on projects that should have taken 30 minutes. Now I'm out the door at 5:00 p.m. I wouldn't be surprised if I got more done in my compressed work-day than when I basically lived at the office.

I've got a reasonably long commute every day (35 to 40 minutes) and I change focus in the afternoons. In the mornings I listen to audio books, business pod casts, or audio Ted talks to fire myself up for the day ahead. In the afternoon, my focus is on winding down and re-entering the human race, so to speak. I either listen to the radio or a personal playlist.

Evenings are for family, and I don't work. I leave my work cell phone in my briefcase. I do briefly check it before bed, but I don't touch it when I'm with my family in the afternoon. I have a separate cell phone that I use for family calls and taking photos. No one else has that number.

Our evening routines change regularly. Sometimes we're at the kids' sporting events several nights a week, other times we're at the movies, out for dinner, visiting or being visited by friends or family, or just spending time at home. I often don't even know what's happening one day to the next. I just go with the flow and enjoy the lack of responsibility in the evenings."

Printed in Great Britain
by Amazon